# Before It Wriggles Away

*by*

## Janet S. Wong

Richard C. Owen Publishers, Inc.
Katonah, New York

# Meet The Author

Text copyright © 2006 by Janet S. Wong
Photographs on pages 4, 5, 6, 7, 13, 15, and 30 right © 2006 by Janet S. Wong
All other photographs copyright © 2006 by Anne Lindsay

Richard C. Owen Publishers, Inc.
PO Box 585
Katonah, New York 10536

Library of Congress Cataloging-in-Publication Data

Wong, Janet S.
    Before it wriggles away / by Janet S.Wong.
        p. cm.—(Meet the author)
    ISBN-13: 978-1-57274-861-3
    ISBN-10: 1-57274-861-3
    1. Wong, Janet S.—Juvenile literature. 2. Authors, American—21st century—Biography—Juvenile literature. 3. Children's literature—Authorship—Juvenile literature.  I. Title. II. Series: Meet the author (Katonah, N.Y.)

    PS3573.0578Z55 2006
    811'.54—dc22
    [B]

                                                                    2006046411


Editor, Art, and Production Director        *Janice Boland*
Editorial and Production Assistant          *Christine Ditmans*

Printed in China

9       8       7       6       5       4       3       2       1

For more information about our collection of Meet the Author books and other children's books visit our website at www.RCOwen.com or call 800-336-5588.

*To my family*

When I was a child, I never thought I would be a poet.
I hated poetry! I never imagined that I would be an author.
I did not love books.

Books were too quiet. Reading was lonely. I liked watching
TV with my dad. I liked hearing my grandfather tell stories.
I liked playing with my friends, riding my skateboard,
and catching lizards.

I grew up in Los Angeles, California. Both of my parents worked. My father was an accountant and my mother was a hairdresser. Many women wore their hair up in tall, fancy hairstyles then. I loved my mother's perfect hair.

I remember feeling very grown-up when she gave me my first curly perm.

I started going to preschool when I was two years old. The preschool was held in a red house owned by an old woman who taught us art and writing and math and German and French. I loved learning German and French. I studied those languages again in high school and college.

My favorite memory of that preschool is of my fourth birthday party. We spent a lot of time having birthday parties.

I had a very happy childhood, but I never imagined that my life would end up being important or exciting enough to write about.

It was just a regular kid's life—wake up, go to school. After school, play with friends. Feed the dog, do homework, eat dinner, watch TV. Sleep. On weekends go to the park or the library. Work in the yard or go for a ride.

One night when I was in high school, I stayed up very late struggling to write an essay for college that would make me sound interesting.

I thought my life was not interesting, but it was.
And because I was a good student, I got into UCLA,
where I studied history.

After college, I went to Yale Law School and became a lawyer.
One summer I worked for legal aid, helping homeless people.
I also worked for law firms and other companies, doing a little
bit of different kinds of law. Sometimes I had to fire people,
which made me feel terrible. Often I felt bored with my job,
buried in stacks of law books and complicated legal
documents. I was making a lot of money, and I love spending
money. But I was *unhappy*!

After four years of being a lawyer, I wanted to do
something different. I wanted to do work that would be
more important. I could not think of anything more
important than working with kids.

One day, I went to a tiny bookstore to shop for picture
books for my young cousin. Next thing I knew,
I had an armload of books that I wanted to buy for *myself*.

I loved those books!

An idea hit me: people wrote those books.
Could I be one of them?  This could be important
work—and it also could be fun!

I didn't know anything about how to write a book
or get it published, but I decided to try writing for a year.

I worked hard at writing.  I read lots of books on how to
get published.  I studied new books to find out
what publishers were looking for.  I took a class
on how to illustrate children's books.  Ruth Bornstein,
the teacher, was an author and illustrator of many books.
She gave me encouragement and hope.

By the end of a year, I had more than two dozen
rejection letters.  I felt like a failure.  I wondered if I was
wasting my time, writing.  I thought about going back to
being a lawyer.  But I *loved* writing, so I kept on doing it.

One of the best things about writing is that you can do it anywhere and anytime. You don't have to get up early and go to an office. But you *do* need to train yourself to write anywhere and anytime, because you never know when an idea will pop into your head. And you have to write it down before it wriggles away.

I often write late at night, after everyone else has gone to sleep. Sometimes I take my laptop and write near the lake.

I got my first book, *Good Luck Gold*, published
a year and a half after I quit my law job. *Good Luck Gold*
is a poetry book. (Over a third of my books are poetry
books.) How did I, a poetry-hater, come to write poetry?

The answer: a great teacher.

After getting those dozens of rejection letters,
I went back to school. I needed to learn how to write
better—to write for children.

Myra Cohn Livingston, the author of more than 80 books
of poetry, showed me that I really didn't know enough
about poetry to hate it. I thought I hated poetry, but
what I hated was studying poems, picking them apart,
trying to find a hidden meaning.

Myra urged me to read lots of different kinds of poems:
funny poems, serious poems, rhyming poems, free-verse,
haiku, and poems that sounded like regular talk.
Her book *Poem-Making* is my favorite book on how
to write poetry.

I had never realized how many different kinds of poems there are. For everything you have seen and done, there is a poem—or a poem waiting to be written! I have written about noodles, ladders, my family, dogs, gardening, saber fencing, chess, and much more.

Every day I find something new to write about!

What do I like best about being an author?

I love talking about my books.  I also enjoy sharing
favorite books written by other authors.  A favorite book
is like a friend.

I have talked about my books in many different places.
Once I was asked to speak at the White House Easter
Egg Roll. Another time I was invited to be part of the
Oprah Winfrey Show. This year CNN, the Cable News
Network, videotaped me speaking in a classroom.

So far I have spoken to over 500,000 children around the world. I have visited schools, libraries, and bookstores in Singapore, Beijing, Hong Kong, Hawaii, California, Washington, Texas, and New York.

Every visit is different. Each classroom has something
wonderful I have never seen before. Each child I meet has
his or her own questions, ideas, and unique stories to tell.

Sometimes I get tired of traveling, of being away from home. It seems as if I spend at least half of each month "on the go," zipping down the freeway, hopping on trains, dashing through airports—and then waiting, waiting, waiting "to get there." Travel, for me, is a lot of "hurry up and wait."

Every now and then I spend two days traveling to a place and back, just to speak for half a day. It would make more sense to spend a whole week or two in one place, visiting many schools. But I don't like being away from my family for too long, so I am always rushing home. Besides, as a mom, I have a lot of things to do!

When I am not traveling to speak about my books or to teach poetry, much of my time is filled with doing the things that moms do.

I shop for apples and toilet paper, bread and light bulbs. I take my son to his fencing lessons. I watch him play hockey.

I also volunteer at my son's school, sometimes making decorations, sometimes sharing my poems in classrooms, sometimes helping with class parties.

I spend a lot of time answering e-mail. I get hundreds of e-mails each day from teachers, librarians, parents, booksellers, reporters, my publishers, and children.

I check my e-mail as often as I can. I love getting good news.

Reading other people's books often inspires me to get going and write something new. I think it's funny that I used to hate reading because it was too quiet. Now I love the quiet of it.

I also love the noisy part of reading—hearing different voices coming alive in my head. I especially love reading in bed on a cold morning, snuggled up cozy with books.

How do I find time to write books?

I do a lot of my writing in little bits. You can
write anywhere and anytime. All you need is a pen
and a scrap of paper.

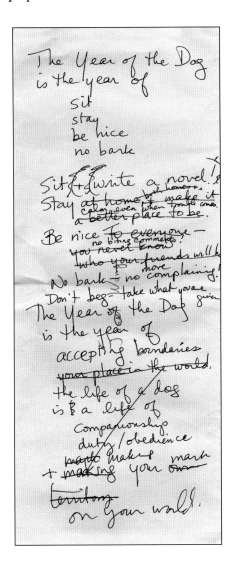

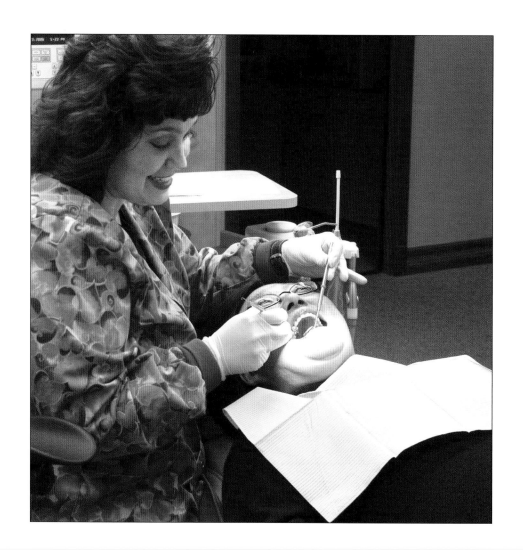

If I get to the dentist's office early, I might write a first draft
of a poem. While my mouth is wide open and I cannot write,
I will let my mind wander. Those "wandering thoughts" are
part of the writing process.

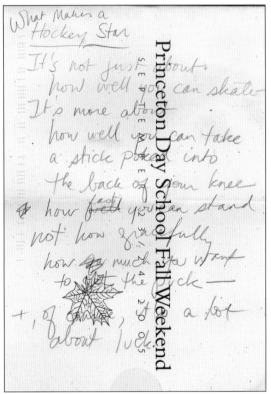

Here is a draft of a poem I wrote while I was waiting in the car for a hockey game to start. (I might work on the poem later, on the computer.)

25

Most of my writing happens on the computer,
where it is easy to delete or add, copy and paste,
and write drafts.

I think of each draft as another chance to win.
It's hard to know, when you're in the middle of writing,
what will "turn out" and what won't. It's impossible to know
if what you're working on will get published. But the more
you write, the better your chances will be.

Sometimes when I write something, I get stuck.

I may like part of it, but don't know how to make it better.

That is why I share my writing with friends.

It's very useful to know what someone likes best

about a piece of writing or what might be confusing about it.

What subjects do I like writing about best of all?

I like writing about my family, my friends, and my everyday life—both sad and happy things, the kinds of things that my teacher, Myra Cohn Livingston, showed me I could write about.

It makes me happy to write about favorite times—driving with my father, eating a *dim sum* lunch with my mother, playing ball with my dog Nissa, spending time with my husband and my son.

I have written about catching lizards, baking cookies
with my grandmother, and about the day I was thrown off
my skateboard and needed thirteen stitches in my chin.

I want to write a book of poems about food,
and another on sports, and a novel about a teen
who gets a traffic ticket that changes her life.

I have so many ideas.  The hard part is to get them
down on paper or in my computer before they disappear.

*Think of a poem*
*as a slippery thing.*

*You need to catch hold,*
*before it wriggles away —*

Happy reading!

# Other Books by Janet S. Wong

*Alex and the Wednesday Chess Club; Behind the Wheel: Poems about Driving; Buzz; Good Luck Gold and Other Poems; Grump; Hide & Seek; Minn and Jake; Night Garden: Poems from the World of Dreams; The Rainbow Hand: Poems about Mothers and Children; A Suitcase of Seaweed and Other Poems; You Have to Write.*

# About the Photographer

Anne Lindsay is an award-winning photographer. She lives in the northwestern state of Washington with her husband Frank, her daughter Fiona, and their dog Alice. In her studio nestled on a lake, Anne creates images for authors, books, and magazines.

# Acknowledgments

Special thanks to: Bev Gallagher and her third graders at Princeton Day School in Princeton, New Jersey, Kelly Crickmore and the students at Sunny Hills Elementary in Sammamish, Washington, Dr. Tonya A. Loving of Loving Dentistry in Issaquah, Washington, Larry's Markets in Seattle, Washington, and to all children and friends pictured in this book. Gratitude to Christina Biamonte of Harcourt, Inc., Agnes Fisher of Simon and Schuster, and Victoria Fox of Farrar Straus Giroux for facilitating permissions for the following covers on page 29. Cover of *This Next New Year* text © 2000 by Janet S. Wong, illustrations © 2000 by Yangsook Choi. Used by permission of Farrar Straus Giroux. Cover of *Knock on Wood: Poems about Superstitions* text © 2003 by Janet S. Wong, illustrations © 2003 by Julie Paschkis. Used by permission of McElderry Books, an imprint of Simon and Schuster. Covers of *Apple Pie 4th of July* text © 2002 by Janet S. Wong, illustrations © 2002 by Margaret Chodos-Irvine and *The Trip Back Home* text © 2000 by Janet S. Wong, illustrations © 2000 by Bo Jia. Used by permission of Harcourt, Inc.